A WEEK IN
THE WHITE HOUSE
WITH

THEODORE

ROOSEVELT

A STUDY OF THE PRESIDENT AT THE NATION'S BUSINESS

BY

WILLIAM BAYARD HALE

1908

Contents

PUBLISHER'S NOTES 6

FOREWORD 8

INTRODUCTORY 9

THE PRESIDENT IN THE WHITE HOUSE..............................12

A VIEW OF THE PRESIDENT AT WORK...............................18

THE SPIRIT OF THE WHITE HOUSE....................................27

A TYPICAL DAY WITH THE PRESIDENT 30

A CABINET DAY AT THE WHITE HOUSE.............................41

GIVING AUDIENCES TO TWO HUNDRED.............................45

AN ESTIMATE OF MR. ROOSEVELT....................................49

THE PRESIDENT ON MR. ROOSEVELT 59

PUBLISHER'S NOTES

THIS is a unique view into the daily White House under one of our most dynamic and fascinating presidents. For one week, William Hale had unfettered access to T.R. and he used the time to great advantage, leaving us with a frank and open account.

The reporter himself was something of an interesting fellow with a controversial past.

William Bayard Hale was born April 6, 1869 in Richmond, Indiana to William Hadley Hale and Anna Catherine Bunting Hale. William was the middle of three children. As an adult, he was tall for his day, reaching six foot two inches.

William attended Boston University and Harvard University before graduating from Episcopal Seminary College in Cambridge. He entered the priesthood, in which he remained for seven years before becoming a journalist in 1900. Hale was the first rector of Church of Our Saviour in Middleborough, Massachusetts, and served from 1892 to 1899. He was apparently influential in getting the church constructed. In 1895, at the age of 26, he traveled abroad alone from his home in Middleborough. He stated his intention to return "before the class of 1895."

In 1908, he interviewed the German Kaiser, Wilhelm II and he published the book you are reading. The writing does not betray any particular agenda towards promoting T.R. who at any rate was near the end of his term and had stated he would not run again. Hale's role here is one of interested observer and analyst.

In 1909, Hale married 26-year-old Olga Unger, a New York City native, in London. Together they had two children.

In 1911, he wrote and published Woodrow Wilson's presidential campaign biography. On Wilson's direction, he went to Mexico to negotiate with José Venustiano Carranza Garza, one of the leaders of the Mexican Revolution and later Mexico's president.

A 1913 report by Hale, as a confidential agent in Mexico, implicated ambassador Henry Lane Wilson in the murder of Francisco Madero by Victoriano Huerta. Wilson recalled the ambassador and the U.S. began a campaign to drive Huerta from Mexico. In 1915, Hale became a propaganda adviser to Germany until the United States entered World War I. His book, *American Rights and British Pretensions on the Seas* (1915), stirred American resentment of the British blockade. In 1917, William Randolph Hearst sent him to Europe as a war correspondent. Denounced and ostracized in the United States, he lived in Europe after the war, which is why he does not appear in census counts for those years.

It's interesting given his controversial status that he had in 1907 applied for membership in the Sons of the American Revolution. He died in Munich, Germany in 1924. He is buried in the crypt of the Church of Our Saviour in Middleborough. Olga returned to the United States and raised her children in New York City.

FOREWORD

Nothing more interesting could be conceived, either for contemporaneous reading or for the purposes of history, than an accurate and realistic picture of the remarkable man who now occupies the Presidential chair as he appears at close hand actually engaged in the great duties of his office.

The following article presents such a picture—the first ever given of any President at his work, and by all odds the most intimate study of Mr. Roosevelt ever made public. The author spent some days watching the progress of Executive business at the White House and has here given a narrative of his observations—so far as consistent with propriety.

IT IS TO BE CLEARLY UNDERSTOOD THAT THE PRESIDENT IS IN NO SENSE AND TO NO DEGREE WHATSOEVER RESPONSIBLE FOR ANY STATEMENT, SENTIMENT, OR OPINION THAT FOLLOWS.

Nor does the author, when quoting the President, pretend to give his exact language; he records merely the impression made.

INTRODUCTORY

IT was curious enough that, on the train to Washington, a well-thumbed copy of the *Journal Intime*—which one may read with safety in the springtime—should have opened of itself so often to passages like these:

The East prefers immobility as the form of the Infinite; the West, movement. It is because the West is infected by the passion of details.... Like a child upon whom a hundred thousand francs have been bestowed, she thinks she is multiplying her fortune by counting it out in pieces of twenty sous, or five centimes. Her passion for progress is in great part the product of an infatuation, which consists in forgetting the goal to be aimed at, and absorbing herself in the pride and the delight of each tiny step, one after the other. Child that she is, she is even capable of confounding change with improvement.

The divine state *par excellence* is that of silence and repose, because all speech and all action is in itself limited and fugitive. Napoleon with his arms crossed over his breast is more expressive than the furious Hercules beating the air with his athlete's fists. People of passionate temperament never understand this. They are sensitive only to the energy of succession; they know nothing of the energy of condensation....

Having early a glimpse of the absolute, I have never had the indiscreet effrontery of individualism. What right have I to make a merit of a defect? I have never been able to see any necessity for imposing myself upon others, nor for succeeding. I have seen nothing clearly except my own deficiencies and the superiority of others. That is not the way to make a career.

If the gentle philosopher of Geneva could have lived to see this day and had looked about for the chief living incarnation and exemplification of the view of life which he reprobated, he would have recognised it in the person of the twenty-fifth President of the Republic whose proclivities he did live to deplore. A fresh reading of the journal of this man of contemplation was, therefore, scarcely the appropriate preparation for a study of the man of action.

9

Nevertheless, however much I may have been impressed with Amiel's* praise of the energy of concentration, after an observation of the President during a number of days I am prepared to admit that there is a place in the world also for representatives of the energy of succession.

*Probably referring to Henri Frédéric Amiel (1821–1881), a Swiss philosopher, poet, and critic.

It is, at all events, certain that the Oriental type of mind is not adapted to the leadership of the Western world. The holy man who spends a lifetime contemplating his navel, may achieve rich stores of wisdom and may free his soul from earthly dross—but he would not make a good President of the United States. If we of the West will persist in our infatuation for movement, then the force of circumstances will push to our head the man who most completely represents activity.

This is the principle which has made Theodore Roosevelt President; which would inevitably have made him President in any conceivable combination of events; this is the principle which has made him far more than President. Think what you may of Mr. Roosevelt's policies—and let it be said now that this article has nothing to do with these—believe him all wrong if you will, hate him personally, if you will, it is impossible to deny that he is the idol of more Americans than any other man has ever been, and that he is believed abroad to be the most typical man of his nation. He is the type of active energy.

Any portrait of Mr. Roosevelt must make that fact prominent. But it is that fact which makes a portrait such as this would be—a "pen portrait" in the old phrase, namely—the only one that can hope to portray him. The President has been studied on the model throne and at his desk by Chartran, Sargent, Rouland,* and others. He will never live in verity on any canvas. Of all men the President lends himself least to portraiture by the brush. Painting is a still art. It cannot represent action. The President in repose is a dynamo at rest—and looks the part. But it is hardly worth while to paint a dynamo. M. Chartran's hand symbolises strength; Rouland's face and pose express strength. But the only picture that can give Mr.

Roosevelt will be drawn by the art of words. They photograph the lightning now, but it is a poor sense of its brilliant energy one gets from the fixed outline of the picture. I believe the cinematograph hasn't yet been prefected to the point where it can catch the flame of heaven, and I am sure it couldn't keep up with Mr. Roosevelt's activity.

It is the hope of this article, however, to give a sort of verbal cinematographic study of the President. It wants to picture him forth in the succession of attitudes and moods through which he passes as he carries on the work of the Nation, and to record the impressions which he makes upon one who observes him in the unconscious self-revelation of his busiest hours. It is to be understood that it is a view of the President at work, a picture of the man in his Executive Office.

Théobald Chartran (1849–1907), French; classical propaganda painter. John Singer Sargent (1856–1925), American; the leading portrait artist of his time. Orlando Rouland (1871-1945), American; portrait painter.

THE PRESIDENT IN THE WHITE HOUSE

IMAGINE, then, a room thirty feet square, with three windows looking south over the White House grounds to the Potomac and the Virginia hills, the top half of the Monument visible over the back-screen of a tennis court. A big desk with a few papers (always in order), a few books, an art nouveau lamp, and two or three vases of flowers, facing a fireplace above which hangs an oil portrait of Lincoln—a poor one; I hope it bears the "pinxit" of no friend of mine. It is the only artistic ornament of the room; though there is a tiny clock on the mantel, and a little above it a photograph of a big bear and a framed autograph of the sonnet by J. J. Ingalls:

OPPORTUNITY

Master of human destinies am I.
Fame, love, and fortune on my footsteps wait,
Cities and fields I walk; I penetrate
Deserts and seas remote, and passing by
Hovel, the mart, and palace, soon or late
I knock unbidden once at every gate!
If sleeping wake—if feasting, rise before
I turn away. It is the hour of fate,
And they who follow me reach every state
Mortals desire, and conquer every foe
Save death; but those who doubt or hesitate.
Condemned to failure, penury, and woe,
Seek me in vain and uselessly implore,
I answer not, and I return no more.

The room contains no patriotic symbol nor emblem of office, unless the big bunch of American Beauties be considered one, and the huge globe in a corner in some sort the other. Besides, a leather-covered divan and a chair or two, mahogany, like the desk. The woodwork ivory, the walls covered with dark olive burlap, two windows behind the desk, five pairs of olive curtains. So severe is the room that very few business men indeed have not its superior in decoration, if not in simple comfort.

There is no telephone in the President's Office.

Adjoining this room and connecting with it by sliding doors, so that the two apartments are practically one, is a counterpart, though ten feet longer—the Cabinet room. This is pretty well filled up by the great table around which the President's advisers assemble on Tuesdays and Fridays at eleven. Each of the arm-chairs is assigned and bears upon its back a silver plate indicating its assignment. I don't know that anybody ever looks up, but if he does he sees in the middle of the ceiling of either room a cluster of electric lights set at the heart of a system of gilded rays where a picture of an All-Seeing Eye might be expected. The President's fauteuil has a back a trifle taller than have the seats of the Executive family. I grieve to state that the Cabinet room harbours a cuspidor. A big divan; half a dozen chairs against the wall, which is adorned only with maps; a pair of dwarf Japanese pines on the mantel, and—it is no time to suppress the truth—frequently the silk hat of a visitor; a revolving book-case containing the Federal Statutes at

Large and such like tomes; a table and a silver water-pitcher in a corner—and you have a picture of the olive-and-ivory office whence go forth edicts which have determined so much contemporaneous history and in so large a measure are shaping the burdened future. For the matter of that I remember that i o, Downing Street is plain, and I have seen a King dispense judgment under a tree and a Pope give blessing in a garden.

But no man has ever seen, anywhere on earth, a scene of such democratic setting and manner of enactment, significant of such far-reaching results, as that which is to be seen in these olive-and-ivory rooms any day when the flag is flying over the White House roof. The President repairs to his office each morning at 9:30, except on Sunday, and to it come to seek him the high and the low—if there be any low in a Republic like this of ours. Before you admit them in imagination get the permanent features of the scene in mind:

Imagine at the desk sometimes, on the divan sometimes, sometimes in a chair in the farthest corner of the Cabinet room, more often on his feet—it may be anywhere within the four walls—the muscular, massive figure of Mr. Roosevelt. You know his features—the close-clipped brachycephalous head, close-clipped mustache, pince-nez, square and terribly rigid jaw. Hair and moustache indeterminate in colour; eyes a clear blue; cheeks and neck ruddy. He is in a frock-coat, a low collar with a four-in-hand, a light waistcoat, and grey striped trousers—not that you would ever notice all that unless you pulled yourself away from his face and looked with deliberate purpose. Remember that he is almost constantly in action, speaking earnestly and with great animation; that he gestures freely, and that his whole face is always in play. For he talks with his whole being—mouth, eyes, forehead, cheeks, and neck all taking their mobile parts. The President is in the pink of condition to-day; his face clear, his weight I should say well-nigh a stone less than was his habit back of a year ago. Look at him as he stands and you will see that he is rigid as a soldier on parade. His chin is in, his chest out. The line from the back of his head falls straight as a plumb-line to his heels. Never for a moment, while he is on his feet, does that line so much as waver, that neck unbend. It is a pillar of steel. Remember that steel pillar. Remember it when he laughs, as he will do a hundred times a day—heartily, freely, like an irresponsible school-boy on a lark, his face flushing ruddier, his eyes nearly closed, his utterance choked with mirth, and speech abandoned or become a weird falsetto. For the President is a joker, and (what many jokers are not) a humourist. He is always looking for fun—and always finding it. He likes it rather more than he does a fight—but that's fun too. You have to remember, then, two things to see the picture: a room filled with constant good-humour, breaking literally every five minutes into a roar of laughter—and a neck of steel.

Not that the President always stands at attention. He doubles up when he laughs, sometimes. Sometimes—though only when a visitor whom he knows well is alone with him—he puts his foot on a chair. When he sits, however, he is very much at ease—half the time with one leg curled up on the divan or maybe on the Cabinet table top. And, curiously, when the President sits on one foot his visitor is likely to do the same, even if, like Mr. Justice Harlan or Mr. J. J. Hill, he has to take hold of the foot and pull it up.

All this may be very idle, yet it is all part of the scene.

Imagine ushered into this olive-and-ivory apartment inhabited by its great personality, a procession of Cabinet Ministers, Supreme Court Justices, Senators, Governors, Representatives,

Mayors, bureau chiefs and departmental officers, political leaders, officers of the Army and Navy, seekers for office (hungry importunate), postmasters, collectors, Federal marshals and attorneys, counsellors, commissioners, delegations representing all conceivable interests, almost all with favours to beg for, men with reports to make, men with grievances to complain of—these interspersed with distinguished citizens, often accompanied by their wives, *literati* from every clime, travellers on globe-girdling journeys who want to shake hands, hunters, cattlemen, railroad presidents, reformers (fire in each eye and papers in each hand) , miners, mechanics, Indians, Japanese, editors, clergymen—all who can get a Congressman to introduce them—imagine such a procession passing from Do till I:30 each day and day after day, and this man dealing with it—as I shall tell.

They are ushered into the Cabinet room, after a longer or a shorter wait in the ante-rooms, by the doorkeeper, Major Loeffler, who, in any other land, would be a personage of recognised influence, though, indeed, his importance is recognised here. For, however democratic, the President's audience-room is a court, and admission to the Presidential presence at the right moment and under favourable circumstances may be the making of a career the most unpromising, or the ruining of one the most lofty. The doorkeeper's watchful eye keeps three or four important personages, or maybe a score of less important ones, in the Cabinet room. Senators and Representatives have the entrée between 10 and 12 o'clock. All others are obliged to arrange a special appointment through Mr. Loeb, Secretary to the President. The doorkeeper admits the latter from his printed list. The privileged enter without awaiting the doorkeeper's invitation, swelling the audience until sometimes there are twenty assembled in the Cabinet room—men the names of half of whom are famous, while those of the other half are unknown save in their village or labour union. It is not always possible to distinguish the pillar of state from the private citizen. One not familiar with the figures who are enacting the drama of the Nation's Administration would find it somewhat difficult to believe that great things are happening in these rooms.

All within the Executive Office await the President's pleasure. The rule may be said to be: You come to the White House for Audience- an interview with the President, but once you are within it, the President goes to you to give you the interview. He does not keep his seat and summon you. He is quite alone and unattended. He may speak your name or beckon. He is more likely to step up to you, greet you, get at your business, dispose of it, say good-bye, and pass to another. In this way he will make the circuit of the Cabinet room half a dozen times of a morning. Here it is a case of "yes" or a "no." Here it is to hear a story and make a reference to the proper department and official. In many instances it is to consider and decide in one minute, on the feet, finally, a matter of importance, often of vast consequence. Now and then the President passes a visitor and returns when he has disposed of half a dozen others to have two whole minutes standing with him in the nearly emptied room. Now and then a Senator or a Cabinet secretary will be motioned into the inner room while the President continues his round, or taken into it while the others wait watching the two at the desk or on the divan. Here is a delegation to be listened to and answered. Here a distinguished citizen to be greeted, merely. Here a patriotic gentleman anxious to serve his country in a remunerative office, to be sent away with any hope there may be for him.

It is a procession, the passing of which affords a panorama of the National life; the look and bearing of which makes one proud of his fellow-countrymen; the reception Panorama of which makes him marvel of the President Life.

I affirm that if any who in these days of cynicism despairs of popular government could spare an hour in the President's room he would leave freshened and sweetened with a sense of the essential worth of American civilisation. Every President has given free audience to representatives of the people. But not before has the Nation been what it is to-day, with its possessions in the antipodes and its influence in every other capital on the globe. And not before has there met the visitors a man like this—a man with a mind so apt and spirit so sincere, without self-consciousness and without reserve, a man of such rarely failing gleefulness and yet such indomitable resolution.

Mr. Roosevelt is always President and always a very strong-willed and assertive President. He will be master or he will die. And yet he will not be master otherwise than by virtue of his ability to prove that he ought to be. He maintains his right to have his way—on the ground that his way is right. He is ready to go into the arena at any moment and fight out all over again the question which is the best man, which is the best cause. He will make no appeal to his Constitutional dignity; he will not dominate by symbolism. He will not say: "I am President; people, bow down." He will say: "I am right on this thing, and you have got to admit it." And it is here in these rooms of olive and ivory that he is forever doing both these things: ruling with an indomitability of will with which no other President and with which scarcely a Ptolemy or a Caesar ever ruled, and all the time freely, with a democracy of spirit impossible to conceive, with good nature, with gallant courtesy, with robust joy, maintaining and vindicating against all corners his right to rule.

A VIEW OF THE PRESIDENT AT WORK

THIS is the manner of it:

A Cabinet secretary is seated in the inner office. A dozen men are standing in the Cabinet room. The President is passing around the table—he never goes, so to speak, "with the bottle" and the hands of the clock, but always in the reverse direction. His speech is explosive, not merely emphatic, and his hand-grip is strong.

Let me say here, what must be kept in mind constantly, that I report the President's words only as I remember them. No record was kept; no notes were taken. Very likely I may have introduced locutions which were not the President's—my own or those of visitors, the impression of which could easily have become confused with that made by the President's words. It would be entirely unwarrantable to hold Mr. Roosevelt responsible for any utterance reported in this manner—nor will any one presume to do so. I believe, however, that the impression I give of the President's words and manner is essentially accurate.

"Senator, I—am GLAD to see you. Senator, this is a—VERY great pleasure. Only to introduce Mr. B? Well, Sir, it is a VERY great pleasure to meet you, Sir, a—VERY GREAT pleasure. You please me by giving me this opportunity. Your daughters? I am, INDEED, pleased to have this visit from you. It is a GREAT PLEASURE. Senator, I THANK you for affording me this opportunity. I lived in Dakota myself before there was a South Dakota and I THOUGHT I knew something of the possibilities of the country. But who would have DREAMED Of this? We thought Dakota had something to boast of in my day, but we hardly hoped for such altogether satisfactory and CHARMING products as THIS! This is a GREAT pleasure, young ladies."

They are indeed pretty girls, but a sad-faced veteran, tall, and still erect with the remnants of military bearing, though he visibly trembles as he supports himself on his stick, is waiting.

You would instinctively address him as, "Colonel." To him the President passes:

"I am VERY glad indeed to see you, Sir. Have you prepared the papers of which I spoke? It would be advisable to lose no time in doing so. The Department is exacting about those matters— necessarily so, you understand. You may depend."

But the old man, between excitement and poor ears, can't follow the President's rapid utterance and throws up a hand in despairing gesture. The President begins again, stepping closer and speaking slowly and distinctly. Still: "I am very sorry, Mr. President, that I don't seem able quite to follow you. I feared it might be this way, and I have the whole thing right here. I have put it all on this paper in the fewest possible words. I have counted the words and can't take one away. It will save you trouble."

That was the only paper the President accepted that day. "Yes," he said, "this is indeed the very best way. I thank you for your KIND consideration of men and the Nation's time. I THANK you, Sir." And the veteran went away, his fingers pretty well used up by a friendly handshake, but his heart warm toward a considerate President.

Next stand a Senator and a Governor with a candidate to succeed Mr. Ridgely as Controller of the Currency. They get little satisfaction.

The Public Printership is on the President's mind. He asks a visitor:

"What do you know about? Taft thinks well of him." Every day some one broaches the matter of the Public Printer to the President. He asks:

"What do you think of? Loeb says that—is a fine fellow. I am trying to find out what the law means by 'a practical printer.' I want somebody there who will stop waste and save money."

An Army officer wants leave of absence. "Send me a memorandum, so that I can take it up on Friday with the Cabinet."

A new Congressman is next in the circle. He pulls out a long letter from the Postmistress of Cement—I think it is in Arizona. The President is visibly torn between impatience and a desire not to hurt the visitor's self-respect.

"My DEAR Sir, you must see that my hands are pretty full here. I really know nothing about this case. You say she has been treated unfairly, she thinks? That is too bad. We can't have injustice done anybody, least of all a woman. Take this matter up with Mr. Meyer. It is his affair first, you know. He may see something of the merits of the case; really, I do not. I have never heard of the good woman, and to be PERFECTLY candid with you, I have never heard of—Cement! I couldn't act any way until after I had had a report from the Postmaster General. That is the way for you to get at it. It is a VERY great pleasure to have seen you and I hope you will COME often. Good-day, Sir."

The President passes on.

Remember that Mr. Roosevelt never speaks a word in the ordinary conversational tone. He utters Affairs Big everything with immense and Little emphasis, his face energised from the base of the neck to the roots of the hair, his arms usually gesticulating, his words bursting forth like projectiles, his whole being radiating force. He does not speak fast, always pausing before an emphatic word, and letting it out with the spring of accumulated energy behind it. The President doesn't allow his witticisms to pass without enjoying them. He always stops—indeed, he has to stop till the convulsion of merriment is over and he can regain his voice.

"My dear Sir, I AM glad to see you. How DARE you introduce yourself to me! I have not forgotten your affair, and you will find that instructions have been given to have your very reasonable request complied with. I wish you good luck, Sir, the very BEST of good luck. It has been a—very—GREAT pleasure to serve you."

"My DEAR Governor, how GOOD of you to come to see me again! I must have more time for you. Wait one moment. Mr. Bartholdt, I am INDEED GLAD to see you."

Representative [Richard] Bartholdt [Republican, Missouri], who is better known as a peace advocate than as a Congressman, has come on a small matter of $90,000,000 for new public buildings. He goes away with the impression that $15,000,000 is about all Congress ought to recommend on the eve of a Presidential campaign.

This is a quiet, almost whispered conference. With the next in the circle the President enters into a subject which arouses him. He bursts out against his detractors. His arms begin to pump. His finger rises in the air. He beats one palm with the other fist.

"They have no conception of what I'm driving at, absolutely NONE. It PASSES BELIEF—the capacity of the human mind to resist intelligence. Some people WON'T learn, WON'T think, WON'T know. The amount of—stupid PERVERSITY that lingers in the heads of some men is a miracle."

The President passes on to Senator Taylor and Representative Hull, and hears what they have to say for their candidate, a Mr. Asbury Wright, for the Tennessee vacancy on the Federal bench.

Then he goes back to the Governor of Nebraska and Senator Burkett and the delegation accompanying them, cattlemen from Nebraska asking the passage of laws that will enable them to lease and fence Government lands for pasturage purposes. It is one of those cases in which 'clamorous class prejudice would detect a conflict between the interest of capital and the interest of the small man. The President sees that and puts the point at once. Senator Burkett has prepared a bill which the delegation declares meets the wishes of the big ranch owners and the little cattlemen; it gives the big herders the chance to range their cattle on Government lands under lease, but allows actual settlers to take up lands whether or not under lease.

The President gives the delegation to understand that he will do everything in his power to help them.

"But the fate of the bill," he adds with a laugh, "lies with the coordinate branch. I am not that, too, all reports to the contrary notwithstanding. But this is precisely what I have been working for and what I stand for, in every branch of the Government—to give the big men and the little men both the best possible chance. Safeguard them equally, too. That is what I have been trying to do in the case of combinations—to encourage good and beneficent combinations and to prevent bad ones. But just as I am handicapped in your matter of the Government lands, which ought not to be permitted to lie idle, which ought to be put to lease under the best conditions possible until the settler who wants them permanently comes along, just so I have been hindered and embarrassed by the ill-devised and foolish and ineffectual anti-trust law which works wrong any way you look at it."

Again let me say that this is an impression from memory, not a record of the President's words.

Then the President goes into the particulars of cattle-raising with the delegation. He knows as much about the subject as any of them. The language of the range is freely on his lips; the special terms and the special knowledge of the ranchman is his in full. He chuckles as he tells the story of a point he had won for the cattlemen over the legislative branch. No matter what—it was a simple affair of slipping a certain provision into an appropriation bill.

"I'm a Western man myself," laughs the President, "and we Western men are quick with our guns. I'd like to have seen Brother's face when he learned the awful truth. Gentlemen, I can't TELL you how GREAT a pleasure this has been. I KNOW your country and I LIKE it. I like the LIFE of it. By George, I do! Let's not forget each other, boys. Good luck to all of you. A great pleasure, a VERY-GREAT pleasure indeed. Governor, take a seat in there with the Secretary."

It is a question not to be decided whether the President or the Nebraskans were the happier during their interview. The President had lectured them on their own subject, told them stories of their own life, and laughed with them till all were convulsed and redder in the face than the prairie sun ever made them. They were good stories, too, and merited the prosperity they would enjoy anyway if they were not worth telling. He had sent them off with a shout of laughter, himself too convulsed to do more than wave a final good-bye.

The President notices a button in the lapel. "Well, comrade, what was your regiment?" is a simple phrase, but it facilitates the hesitating speech of an embarrassed visitor.

A Spanish war hero has a concern he wants to lay before the President. A rosette gives the clue as to his Army experience. "What is your rank, comrade? ONLY a Captain? Why do you say ONLY a

Captain? You ought to be THANKFUL you ARE only a Captain. Don't envy any officer who has higher rank," says the Commander-in-Chief earnestly. "I was overjoyed to be a Lieutenant-Colonel, because it gave me a chance to get to the front."

The President does like the military life. He does not regard his experience during the Spanish War as an episode by the way. He is very proud of it. Still, when the other day a young woman lately back from an excursion to Havana innocently asked him if he had ever been in Cuba, the legendary author of *Alone on San Juan Hill* laughed as uproariously as anybody could. I presume the President has about as much military experience as Colonel Washington had when he was chosen to command the Continental Army. If that does not give him the right to call a Civil War veteran "Comrade," perhaps the fact that he is constitutional Commander-in-Chief may suggest to the President this way of greeting a veteran with a pleasant compliment.

Here is a delegation from the Philadelphia Board of Trade, introduced by Representative McCreary. Another jolly greeting, but the matter is not happy. The League Island Navy Yard is discharging men and shortening the time of others. The President would like to see the mechanics kept employed by the Government, but it is a case of short appropriations.

"I am not the 'co-ordinate branch,'" he says, "much as I sometimes wish I were, much as I sometimes wish I could go down the Avenue and tell some of those people how to vote. We hope to do better by Philadelphia both in the matter of work for the navy-yards and workmen in the army stores. But that is subject to the will of Providence and Uncle Joe. Let me see, did I mention Providence first? I heard someone advising the other day that the President lie down on Uncle Joe. That man didn't know Uncle Joe. Well, gentlemen, go see Taft. Tell him you came at my request and that I want him to do anything that can be done legitimately."

Don't imagine that there is ever any lack of emphasis. This is only the substance of it, but in fact it is all gone over substantially. Don't imagine either that the jokes are casual only. You don't smile with

Mr. Roosevelt; you shout with laughter with him and then you shout again while he tries to cork up more laugh, and sputters,

"Come, gentlemen, let us be serious. This is most unbecoming. And there are Senators present, wise and grave men. Only when I think of my sins against the co-ordinate branch "—and everybody is off again, including the Senators.

A member of the Philadelphia delegation had had good hunting in Northern Pennsylvania last Winter. The President is eager to hear about it, but grows suspicious at the suggestion that he try it himself.

"Come up to Pike County and have a shot? Ah! I know precisely how it would be. I shouldn't get a shot, and I should be told that I should have come last year or next month, or that game was plenty just over the border in the next county! Why, I spent twelve days last winter getting one bear. Twelve days!"

"And now I must get over and see the next President," says a visitor. "Yes, go see Taft," the President responds instantly without a quiver of eye or mouth.

All this has taken perhaps ten minutes, and now the President joins the Secretary of Agriculture, who introduces the members of the Pure Food Advisory Board.

Then there are two minutes with Governor Sheldon on the Currency Relief bill and the Republican prospects in Nebraska.

The Attorney General enters. I had thought the President couldn't listen. It is a mistake. He can listen to the drawl of Mr. Bonaparte; listen to the high-voiced protestations of Secretary Wilson; listen to the man from the other side of the world, who may have tucked away about him somewhere a piece of new knowledge or a new idea; listen gravely to the utterances of the spokesmen of a delegation, and reward him with a beaming smile which confesses that it was as well said as if the President had said it himself. The President can do another thing; he can bring his interlocutor back to the subject with a word. And he can make an inquiry that opens up the heart of the whole matter. I was much impressed by the keenness of the President's questions.

If there is jocularity, there is plenty of seriousness too. It would be killing business without the relief of fun. The President has grown in suavity of manner, and his good-humour has deepened. He is by nature severe—he is severe with himself—and he is masterful; but he has learned to find recreation in the indulgence of a sense of the ridiculous, and he has grown kindlier. His talent for order surprised me. He never looks at the clock, but he seems to have a subconscious sense of the passing of the minutes. He takes up a new man with a new interest like a machine grabbing a new piece of metal to shape it to the requirement in precisely so many seconds. He works off a crowd as if by the stop-watch. Not a second is lost. He sees with eyes fitted by nature with a wide-angle lens, commanding the whole room at once, but intent on the eye of the man to whom he is talking. When at his desk he is signing a document, or putting his "O.K." on an order, or writing an hour or a name in a blank schedule of appointments, during the second while his new vis-à-vis is settling himself or reaching into his pocket for a paper. A noiseless secretary comes in every few minutes and gathers up the proofs of this unobserved work. There isn't an usher nor a master of ceremony nor an attendant nor a guard within the two rooms, yet every man is seen in proper order, under the briskest but seemly conditions, and his affair dispatched swiftly, yet with ample opportunity for its complete airing (I can't too strongly declare that if any man fails to get a full hearing it is his own fault)—all with a good-humour, a frankness, an eager purpose to have everything clear, and a practical efficiency that would be wonderful in any hard-headed business man. This is the paranoiac of his irresponsible accusers; the man who, some have not scrupled to hint, is a dipsomaniac, a cigarette fiend, and a victim of pathological ego enlargement.

One morning a little girl had come in with the last delegation of the day. Her mother had cunningly put an autograph album in her hands against the case of her attracting the President's attention. She did attract it, and so did the album. The big man took it, turned to its front page, and found the kiddie's name—"Rosalie," I think it was—carried it over to the Cabinet table, sat down in his big chair and wrote an affectionate sentiment on a leaf that will probably be preserved for grandchildren to read. Then he had time enough to go back to his own desk for a flower, poking about over three or four bouquets, and picking out an especially pretty white carnation to charm her with a moment before he sent her away with a gleeful shout of possession. Somehow one can't dread with overwhelming fear the dark designs of a man who sits with his legs curled under him and bothers to pick just the right flower for a little girl.

THE SPIRIT OF THE WHITE HOUSE

THAT is the way it goes—not that this is more than a hint of it, or carries the least suggestion of the big things that are going on but cannot be referred to here. It is the most wonderful scene in the world. It is the greatest exhibition that has ever been given of democracy and of power. This mingling of Senators and Justices with cattlemen and railroad mechanics in the audience-room of the head of a nation is a thing to ponder on, and the Spirit of when you consider that he is the most autocratic spirit the Republic has seen in power and yet behold him do more homage to the rights of democracy and magnify them beyond any predecessor, the wonder becomes a phenomenon for history to resolve.

President Roosevelt is a ruler. We don't use the word in this country, and don't like it. But we have the fact—and it is evident we do like it. No European sovereign rules as Roosevelt rules. But he does it by sheer force of character—and let us save our faces by adding, by the consent and desire of the people, who believe him to be right in what he demands. He doesn't do it (this is my point here) by bringing into play any mysterious power inherent in his office. He doesn't do it by surrounding himself with the circumstance of supreme power. He is *primes inter pares* by virtue of a grim determination to be, assisted by a sincerity and perspicacity such as political opposition has never before met and now does not know how to meet. The President is imperious because he thinks he is right. He will meet all corners, on the ground without handicap, and have it out fairly, and maybe hotly. There is just this much formality about it: everybody says "Mr. President," and everybody rises when the President does. There is all proper decorum, but it is the decorum that is observed among gentlemen everywhere. In the midst is the Executive "Chair" of the patriotic orators; if there be any reality corresponding to that pleasing symbol, it is the leather throne from which the President presides over his Cabinet. This is daily a receptacle for the overcoats of private gentlemen, and now and then its arm provides a seat for a story-telling Congressman. To-day the most masterly President of history is in the White House—but the Presidential manner is absent. There is a President who shakes his forefinger and brings his hand down on the table, but one who never patronises or draws back into the robes of his office, one who is candid always and with everybody to the point of indiscretion, who plainly has warm feelings, personal feelings, too, and breaks out with them occasionally—though he exercises far, far more patience than he has ever been given credit for.

These two points I may not return to (they are not picturesque), but I want to emphasise them now: Mr. Roosevelt's *Patience* and his *Orderliness*. Nothing surprised me more. He is called on daily to suffer fools, if not Humour, gladly, at least with resignation, and he has learned to do it. In dealing with men not fools, also, the President has, I think, learned a large measure of forbearance. I fancy that the scrutiny of his public acts in the light of his private reasons would show that he is not the impetuous man we have conceived him. If I do not mistake, he has cultivated control of his temper. I have very good reason indeed to recollect a scene of four years ago when the thunder was loose in the White House and—but this is a study of the President as he is to-day.

The popular idea of him scarcely credits the President with the possession of a sense of order. It is, in point of fact, one of his most marked characteristics. His mind is orderly; its contents are thoroughly arranged; his workshop is scrupulously neat. The division and subdivision of his day is the perfection of system. He goes through every day on a time-table which a railroad engineer could follow no more sharply. His sense of the importance of time is the basis of his fondness for railroad men.

The President's good-humour and candour have not been sufficiently appreciated. It is good to have a President with a laugh like Mr. Roosevelt's. That laugh is working a good deal too; hardly does half an hour, seldom do five minutes go by without a joyful cachinnation from the Presidential throat. When Secretary Taft comes in, there isn't room in the White House for any sound other than the chortling laughter of two big men. The Secretary's laugh is a "Ha! ha! ha! ha!" with a definite and ascertainable number of paroxysms. The President's is a succession of chuckles—a sort of mitrailleuse discharge of laughs. The fun engulfs his whole face; his eyes close, and speech expires in a silent gasp of joy. It is clear that both men get a lot of fun out of life.

For you get no conception of the scene unless you understand that the business of State is constantly relieved with anecdote and good-humour. It is carried on in that spirit, without any reservations, with no uneasiness of conscience, with intentions as light as day and as care-free. There isn't any secrecy about the place. There isn't a back stairway, nor a side door, nor yet a closet in the place. A clothes-pole serves for the ministerial wardrobe.

This is the marvel.

"I couldn't do it otherwise," the President said to me when I expressed my astonishment at the candour and publicity that prevailed. "I couldn't and I wouldn't. I don't know any other way. I rest everything on the righteousness of my cause. Other Presidents have been less candid? Then they were abler men than I am. I can't, simply can't keep any secrets. I can work only in the open daylight and before the sight of men."

A TYPICAL DAY WITH THE PRESIDENT

LET us follow the President through a typical day in the Executive Chamber. To avoid any doubt as to its being really a definite day, I will say that it is Thursday, March 26th.

The President enters his office at 9:25. Five minutes later Secretary Loeb, who has been on hand for half an hour, comes into the President's room with a bundle of mail. The President runs over it and rapidly dictates replies; most of his correspondence, however, he gets rid of in the afternoon. At 9:50 the Secretary of War stalks in and is greeted with a shout. Business of the correspondence sort languishes. The doors connecting the Cabinet room are closed, but Senators are gathering. Mr. Beveridge* comes in, his rapid stride overtaking Mr. [Porter J.] McCumber of North Dakota. The Senator from Indiana is worried: what with a diplomatic embarrassment, a crisis with Venezuela, and the Civic Federation bill sent to the wrong committee, Mr. Beveridge is anxious for the Administration.

*The movie-star-handsome Senator Alberto Jeremiah Beveridge (1862–1927) of Indiana was an historian. He was an intellectual leader of the Progressive Era, and a biographer of Supreme Court Justice John Marshall and President Abraham Lincoln.

However, he has come to put out his hand and steady the ark. "Isn't it a shame, Mack," cries Beveridge, half seriously, "that we should have to waste our time here, we Senators of the United States, waiting for a President!" Presently the Indiana statesman is joined by Congressmen Overstreet and Charles Landis, one of three brothers who sustain in Federal offices in this generation the reputation of a remarkable family. Indiana is always a lively subject. Yesterday Senator Hemingway was here. They are getting their final instructions before going West into the fight. While they wait, Beveridge—deep on his front engraven deliberation sits, and public care—urges Landis to give himself to the raising of red pigs; the Durrack Jersey porker multiplies faster, lives on less, and is better meat than any other breed. All Indiana is devoting itself to the red pig. Before Secretary Taft leaves there has been some serious conversation, but the Indiana statesmen warm up the atmosphere.

Before they go they stand up in a row and take a solemn oath never to divulge a Presidential joke which has been passed around in writing. The President on his part indorses on the back of the memorandum of his wit the words: "To be recalled under no circumstances."

If this record gives any idea that the jocularity in the President's office The Wilfley is excessive or unseemly, it Case Comes is time to correct that impression.

When a Representative from Michigan appeared on an errand, of the issue of which he was probably unsuspicious, there was no fun going. The gentleman is a member of the sub-committee of the House Judiciary Committee, which the day before had reported on the case of Judge Wilfley* of the United States Court for China at Shanghai. The conditions at Shanghai are notorious. Taking advantage of the extra-territoriality provisions, every species of vice and corruption has flourished under the pretence of American legalisation. Judge Wilfley was sent to Shanghai to clean it up. He is not precisely a kid-gloved man. A sweet and gentle soul would hardly be adapted to meet the case. The Judge has, of course, made bitter enemies, and they have pursued him to Washington, demanding his impeachment. A clique in Congress, headed by Representative Waldo of New York, is fighting him. The sub-committee's report was ambiguous, but pointed to a censure of Wilfley. The caller had signed that report.

*Lebbeus Redman Wilfley (1866–1926) served as Attorney General of the Philippines and as a judge of the United States Court for China. The New York Times stated that, as Wilfley had no obligation to follow the strictures of the constitution or local law, there were many complaints by American expatriates, especially one by Lorrin Andrews, former Attorney General of the Territory of Hawaii, who charged that Wilfley had voided a will by a Catholic person because of his prejudice against that church. Wilfley resigned at the end of 1908 and returned to the U.S.

Inasmuch as this incident was the subject of a debate in the House of Representatives on Friday, March 2 7th, I have no hesitation in recounting it here. The charge was made in Congress by Mr. John Sharp Williams, Democratic leader, that the President had violated

Section Six of the First Article of the Constitution of the United States, which provides that no Representative of the people shall be called on to account in any other place for his utterance in Congress. The minority leader added that the forefathers had inserted that clause "because it had been the habit of George III. of England to call to the King's palace Members of Parliament and berate them because of their votes in Parliament, or when Members of Parliament called upon other business to take advantage of the visit to berate them and to class them as King's friends or no King's friends."Mr. Williams promised that, if the evidence showed that the member of whom I write had been called to account by the President, he would propose that the House examine whether or not there had been on the part of the President a breach of the privileges of Congress.

This is what happened: The Representative had come to the White House that morning to introduce the Governor of his State. The President exchanged a few words with the Governor, pleasantly enough, and then turned suddenly to the Congressman, and without parley addressed him, as nearly as I can remember, thus:

"I want to know, Sir, how you could put your name to a report which does rank injustice to a capable and honest official, striving his best to do his duty amidst most untoward conditions! I want to know what you were thinking of to condemn a Judge without giving him a hearing! This is a clear case of vile conspiracy against an upright and a fearless man who is serving his country in a place of danger and hard work. Your report has sent joy to the hearts of the corruptionists of the city where he sat and judged in uprightness. It has put a deeper stain, even than that which rested there before this man began to scrub it out, upon the American flag in the Far East. It has made it harder for this Administration to uphold abroad the good name of the Nation. It is a most outrageous act. Nothing more unfortunate could possibly have happened. You have done a wrong to American interests that it will take years to right—if it can ever be righted. The conditions against which this man fought are notorious. He went there for the purpose of confronting them, and his brave stand has been supported—by whom? By those from whom he had a right to suspect support? By the Congress? No. You have made it possible for them to say over there: 'Oh, yes, while Roosevelt is in office, or while Root is in office, American Judges who do justice abroad will be protected. But when they go out, everything will go back to where it was before. The Administration is not supported by the body of American people.'"

The Representative attempted to defend himself by urging that the reference to his committee allowed no other report. The sub-committee was asked to determine simply whether on the evidence submitted a *prima facie* case had been made out. The report distinctly stated that it was based on this reference and stated furthermore that Judge Wilfley had not been heard in his own defence.

The President was not mollified in the least. He understood all that. That, Mr. Waldo indeed, was precisely the point. It was the committee's duty to decline to make a report on such grounds. It was the committee's duty to say that the conditions of the reference were impossible and might lead to the condemnation of an innocent man, and that it therefore declined to report, on the ground that it did not have the facts in its purview.

"To send forth to the world a report like this is a most cowardly and outrageous thing. I will say nothing of the attitude of Mr. Waldo. His attitude is beyond, beneath, discussion. I cannot trust myself to speak of it. But I must say I cannot see, Sir, how you could put your name to a piece of rank injustice like this. You are a man. Suppose this were a case in which the good name of a woman were involved. Would you sign a report on a hypothetical question? Would you stamp the name of that woman forever with an official declaration that, if the facts were as they were alleged to be, though it had to be admitted she had had no opportunity to offer evidence tending to prove her honour, she was an evil woman? You know you wouldn't. The temper of the American people would not stand for such a thing. The good name of a woman is a jewel to be guarded with extremest care. Shall we be more jealous of anything than of the good name of America in the other hemisphere? I tell you the thing is outrageous."

The President's manner was stern in the extreme; his language was scathing, yet he did not lose his temper. His attitude and bearing was that of one administering a rebuke as to the justice and necessity of which there could be no doubt—as, indeed, there can be no doubt. Mr. Roosevelt's speech is plain, precise Anglo-Saxon.

He is never profane. He never employs a locution unsuitable to the drawing-room. And yet when he likes he can concentrate more imprecatory emphasis in a polite characterisation than most men can in a frenzied curse.

Upon the challenge of Mr. Williams in the House of Representatives on the following day, the Representative gave a sugar-coated account of the episode. His story was that "the President had intimated that he felt that the committee might have expressed itself in a happier manner!"

A land owner from Australia is introduced.

"Let me see," says the President. "You are from. Northeast Australia? Would that be the region of the —" the President names an Australian river. "Farther north? Still your country is tolerably well watered. I need not tell you that I am tremendously interested in Australia—and in New Zealand too. You have one of the most interesting of the newer countries. It is tremendously important that you should avoid one pitfall, however. It is most necessary that something should be done to populate your vast stretches of country. It would be most unfortunate if your cities were to continue to grow out of all proportion to the growth of your farm lands and pasture lands. That always indicates an unhealthy condition, upon which permanent prosperity may not hope to rest. You do well to be proud of Melbourne, Sydney, Adelaide, Dalgety, Brisbane, and Perth—but what are you doing to persuade people to go to your lands? We are very proud of Seattle, Tacoma, Spokane, and Olympia." (The Australian had been introduced by a Washington Senator; in the meantime three other gentlemen had entered the Cabinet room.) "But it won't be any advantage to Washington to allow them to grow faster than the country grows. Why, when Kentucky, from which State these gentlemen come, had the population which the State of Washington has to-day, it didn't

34

contain within its borders a single town of 4000 population." The Kentuckians had learned something of the history of their State, but they nodded and looked at each other, gravely assenting to the correctness of the President's information. He was rushing on into a discussion of dry farming and of the various types of water-traps adapted to a region such as North Australia. "However," he finished, "if you have, as you say, sixteen inches of rainfall, you are pretty well fixed by nature."

Then a South American Consul General appears, with the Republican leader of Virginia and another patriotic Virginian. The Consul General wants a diplomatic appointment, or at the least wants to go to Japan with his present rank. The other Virginian has his eye on an Assistant Commissionership for the Tokio Exposition. The plea is artful; Virginia has only four Federal office-holders; but the Republican party there is united and progressive, and is even talking about carrying the State. There is some frank discussion, in the course of which the President tells of the only diplomatic appointment that is open, and it is really promised to Indiana, if that State has the man for it. The Virginia leader is a very young man, who has been gradually recognised in place of his father. The President tells his friends that new conditions call for new methods, and that young men are better adapted to the leadership of the South to-day than men of another generation.

The President's way when he refuses an application varies from "I doubt, Sir, whether your friend is QUITE the best man for the place, from the information which reaches me. They tell me he is a crook."

Everybody has gone but one quiet man who has been standing near the window in the Cabinet room.

It is Governor [Wilford Bacon] Hoggatt of Alaska. To him now the President goes. "Well, Governor, how is Alaska? Who is killing whom now?" The President's tone is jocular, but his face grows hard as flint as he peruses a 500-word telegram which the Governor hands him. "This is bad. What savages! I suppose you want the troops?" There has been a desperate strike on at the famous Treadwell Mine in Southeastern Alaska. Some of the 1400 strikers, the telegram relates, have stolen dynamite, and it is believed that they will use it. The President remembers that Fort William Henry Seward is only a few hours' distance from Treadwell by steamer.

The President leans against the Cabinet table, and then sits on it, ruminating, rubbing his forehead, looking out the window at the opening japonicas. "I hate to see our troops used in this way. I suppose there is no way out." Governor Hoggatt assures him that he knows of none. The Governor says: "You couldn't get together in all Alaska ten men to fight this crowd. Surely the Government is bound to protect life and property threatened in this way." Then he goes into a history of the Alaska labour troubles, the importation of the Slav miners, the danger to all business enterprise in the Territory if order is not maintained. He is a man with a quiet, assured, even voice, completely master of every fact, every name, and every date. The necessity of military action would seem to be clear enough, but the President is extremely reluctant. Every particle of self-assertiveness has vanished from his bearing, his words, and his manner of speech.

"It is bad business—bad business. I do want to be sure that every resource of the civil power has been exhausted before an appeal is made to the military arm." He sighs, gets up, and walks across the room twice. "I don't see why these enterprises should ever have been begun up there in a region of lawlessness. Well, Governor, go over to the War Department and tell them from me that in case they believe it absolutely necessary they may send troops from Fort Seward. If they believe there is no other way, mind. You believe it absolutely necessary, Governor? "

The President remains silent for a moment longer, sitting on the Cabinet table, staring out of the window. The Governor of Alaska has gone to carry the President's order to send the regulars to the Treadwell Mine. Spring has renewed its attack on Washington this morning, and the White House trees and boscages are bursting out in tender greens. Before the door there is a solitary policeman engaged in upholding the dignity of the approach to the President— and in playing with a squirrel which has climbed to his shoulders.

Visitors are pressing in again. The President engages in a long and serious discussion with Mr. Milton Purdy, the trust-breaking expert of the Department of road Men. Justice Mr. Purdy is likely to be the next United States District Judge of Minnesota, Judge William Lochren having announced his intention to resign. Senator Nelson favours Mr. Hale, a Minneapolis lawyer, but he is sixty-four years old, and the President has a fondness for young men.

The President sees Representative Hepburn over the bill he has introduced to amend the Sherman anti-trust jaw. The President is disappointed at the reference of this bill to the Judiciary Committee of the House. He sees Senator Burroughs of Michigan, talks with Senator McCumber, with Congressmen Weeks, Tirrell, and Gillett, and Bennett and Edwards of Kentucky, and the Second Assistant Postmaster General.

While the President is conferring with the expert trust prosecutor, Mr. [James] J. Hill comes in and takes a seat.

The President waves his hand at the railroad magnate. "See you in just a minute, Mr. Hill." But it is nearer fifteen minutes. "Here is a man," he says as he clasps Mr. Hill's hand, "who I was very much surprised yesterday to learn was such a radical that I saw myself shrunken into a timid weakling of a conservative of the mildest type." The two sit with legs curled up under them on the sofa and shake their fingers at each other's noses. Mr. Hill is not an optimist just now.

A party of railroad engineers who are in Washington conferring with Southern railroads about reduction of wages is seen next. The President wins them at once, but he won't commit himself. "I will do what I can. One thing you can depend on: I won't say I will do a thing until I'm sure that I can come pretty near doing it."

Then there is an interlude of friends paying respects. "I AM glad to see you." "This CERTAINLY is a pleasure." "It was MIGHTY good of you to come and see me. I am really DEEPLY obliged to you." "Now, do you know that NOTHING could be greater pleasure than this?" "By George, I AM glad to see you!" "That's fine. That's bully." "I'm MIGHTY glad to have a chance to see you." "By George, this IS great!"

One of those whom he greets is Senator [Isaac] Stephenson of Wisconsin, who is seventy-nine years old and is president of twenty-five business companies, and who works, so he says, from seven o'clock in the morning until nine o'clock at night. All the same he doesn't interest the President as much as does George L. Sheldon, Governor of Nebraska. The Governor enjoyed himself so much yesterday that he is back again. Governor Sheldon is a young chap, with a still younger look, six feet tall and a trifle over-nourished, with a fine head of hair and a slight stoop. You can see that he was the favourite orator of his class at college. Beveridge looked just that way ten years ago. The Governor gazes about with a satisfied sense. He is in the presence of the paraphernalia of Presidential power—stranger things have happened than that he should one day be there as master. And indeed there is that chance. If Governor Hughes gets the nomination in June, nothing would be more natural than that Nebraska's Governor should be his running mate. But Governor Hughes isn't going to get the nomination, and Sheldon is for Taft. It would be a thing unusual to have both candidates from the West, but Governor Sheldon believes it possible to lick Bryan in his own State.

The President plainly likes the tall young Governor. Apparently he considers that, as Doctor Johnson said of a Scotchman, much may be made of a Nebraskan orator if caught young. The scene reminds one of another, which the late Jeremiah Curtin used to describe. He visited the White House with Governor Greenhalge of Massachusetts in 1891—Mr. Harrison was President then—and found a Civil Service Commissioner pacing the anteroom. "That man," said Greenhalge to Curtin, "looks for all the world as if he had been inspecting the White House, and, having found it suitable, has resolved to come here to live himself." "Yes," replied the translator of Sienkiewicz, "nothing human is more certain than that Theodore Roosevelt will be President." Whatever George L. Sheldon may be, he will never be a Roosevelt, however. He will never talk like this:

"That was a GREAT ride I had yesterday—simply GREAT, I WISH you had been with me. Took two fences, and a water jump, and an embankment—well, I don't know what the grade was, but it was practically perpendicular. You can go down and look at it if you want to. My horse did his prettiest yesterday. General Bell was along. No, no accidents yesterday. I have had my share, though. Let 's see: I've broken my arm, and my rib, and my nose, and my wrist—you see it's a little out of kilter yet—and I've been knocked senseless at polo, and been thrown—well, I don't like to say how many times. No man can strike a prairie dog town without getting into trouble. I recollect one fall I had in that country. I was wound up in my horse and a steer in a manner I shan't forget to my dying day, and was thrown—I thought at the time it was about fifty feet. Governor, I DID enjoy that speech of yours; all but the first part. That was a clear case of misdirected enthusiasm, but the part about Taft was ALL RIGHT."

The President's devotion to out-of-door exercise is, of course, well known. Two afternoons in the week, as a rule, he rides; two afternoons, as a rule, he spends on the tennis court. Clad, this season of the year, in a black sweater, which comes off when the Presidential temperature rises, with a hat pulled over his eyes when he plays in the east court against the sun, when in the west court bare-headed, with Alford W. Cooley or Gifford Pinchot as a partner, he confronts perhaps most frequently the nimble Ambassador of France, James R. Garfield, Robert Bacon, or Herbert Knox Smith. A guest is always particularly welcome at the White House who can put up a good game of tennis. The President's vim and his agility of foot and wrist testify to his excellent form to-day—the result of his careful habits.

Two days a week, as a rule, Mr. Roosevelt goes on a tramp, most frequently along the Potomac. It is whispered that he leads some of his companions a pretty chase—for few people at Washington keep themselves in training as does the President. The other day he was accompanied by Mr. Richard Kearton, an English ornithologist and photographer of wild birds, and the excursion was in Rock Creek park, through the valley and up and down the cliffs. There the two nature-lovers watched the flashing, through the young green of spring-touched boughs, of kingfisher, cardinal, and redwing, robin, bluebird, and Carolina wren, but listened in vain for the note of the mocking-bird, which the Englishman had never heard.

Mr. Roosevelt is the first President who has had time for exercise and play—and one reason he has time for a hundred features of work indoors which no other President ever did is because he takes time for recreation out of doors.

A CABINET DAY AT THE WHITE HOUSE

FRIDAY was Cabinet day, but the President managed to attend to a few small matters: He considered and he declined to grant a pardon in the case of an offender from Texas; he called the Surgeon General of the Army to take under special consideration the case of a young officer turned down because he was declared to have, though he denied it, symptoms of tuberculosis; he made the final arrangements for sending troops to the seat of trouble in Alaska; he gave an unencouraging hearing to a proposition from Oregon (I fancy Mr. Harriman's small Italian was in it); he considered candidates for the position of United States Attorney for the Idaho District—the seat of the trouble culminating in the murder of the Governor of Idaho; he accepted the resignation of the Controller of the Currency, bade the retiring incumbent good-bye, and announced his successor; he received delegations from Tennessee on the matter of the appointment of a Federal Judge for the Eastern District; he dodged a well-planned coup intended to draw him again on the third-term question; he gave some necessary orders for the fleet, now on the greatest maritime expedition in history; he at last reached a conclusion as to the delicate and important subject of the attitude of the Government toward the Government of Venezuela; he determined the Government attitude on the Ambassadorial perplexity surrounding the appointment of Mr. Hill to the Court of the German Kaiser,—and then he convened the Cabinet.

Senator Frazier of Tennessee early brought in a delegation of railroad A Tennessee men. The President was Delegation pleased. "You are a conductor, I think," he said to one a trifle the superior in address. "Now, which is the engineer and which the fireman? Ah, yes. I am an honorary fireman myself," he said, and then he mentioned the names of two or three locomotive engineers, John Still of Atlanta being one, and a fireman or two, and asked his visitors if they knew them.

"We are here, Mr. President," said the spokesman, "in behalf of Foster V. Brown of Chattanooga. I speak in behalf of the unanimous sentiment of the railroad men of Tennessee in declaring our belief that he is the man for the place." And so on. It was that Federal Judgeship. The President heard them through. Then he said:

"Gentlemen, I thank you for coming to see me. This is most important. What you tell me is to be considered very seriously, very seriously indeed. Of course I take it you understand that no plea on behalf of your friend, or of anyone else, would have any weight with me, if it were merely on the ground that the appointment would please any particular class. It is pleasing to me to know that Mr. Brown is liked by the railroad men of Tennessee, if that is an indication that he is esteemed also by every other class and sort and rank of men there, men of every other trade and profession. You don't come here to ask me to appoint Mr. Brown because you think he would be favourable to you." The foreman of the delegation had made a speech not quite of the most discreet sort.

"You wouldn't dream for a moment of hoping that I would do a thing like that; you wouldn't want me to do a thing like that. A judge who would favour his friends in a good cause would be just as corrupt a judge and would work the same harm to our institutions as a judge who would favour those who had corrupted him in an evil cause. The thing to be considered about the man in whose interest you come here is not whether he is wanted by the railroad workingmen or by the capitalists or by the learned, but whether he is an honest, God-fearing, upright man, with the learning and poise for a judge.

"I believe I have said somewhere that it would be desirable if our judges could be drawn more directly from the ranks of men in the activity and struggle of life. This is an hour when the academic must give way to the wise and the practical. There is always perhaps a danger that our judges should grow away from the people, getting out of knowledge of and sympathy with the man who works with his hands. That would be most unfortunate. But it would not be anything like so unfortunate as it would be to make a man a judge simply because the men who work with their hands would like to see him judge. No, the question is, Is he decent, honourable, square, and able? I have heard nothing against your candidate, except that his health is not all that it might be. How about that?"

The Senator from Tennessee assured the President that Mr. Brown's health was satisfactory. As the delegation departed Mr. Frazier lingered a moment. "Boys," cried the President, "he is trying to hand me another man!"

An influential citizen from Vermont with an attractively gowned wife was introduced by his Congressman. The Vermonter had to Work a shot ready; his little speech closed thus: "Mr. President, is it just and right that one man should dictate who shall or who shall not be President?" His face shaped to symbolise righteous indignation at the bare thought, the Vermonter paused for the President's reply. Singularly enough, the impetuous Mr. Roosevelt would not to the breach; the orator's climax remained uncapped. Maybe the President had met the trick before. At all events, the rhetorician had to conclude himself. "No, Sir; it is not. Then no one man can be permitted, not even yourself, Mr. President, to say that Theodore Roosevelt shall not be the next President of the United States."

The President's expression of thanks for the call was made to the wife.

A committee from New York City begging the President to make an address on Memorial Day at Grant's Tomb, one of the great occasions of the patriotic year, was disposed of in twenty words. "Can't, gentlemen. Simply can't. I'll write to you mighty polite, but I can't. Go ask Taft." A Congressman with this delegation (I believe it was Calder of New York) had a word to say for a candidate for Assistant Appraiser of merchandise at New York, but the President had another man in mind.

The Controller of the Currency, William B. Ridgely, handed the President his resignation, and bade him farewell.. His father-in-law, Senator Cullom, and Senator Hopkins came with Mr. Ridgely to ask the President to appoint a Mr. Smith of Illinois to the succession. The President was understood to intimate that the Secretary of the Treasury had expressed himself very forcibly about this appointment, and he regarded it as vitally necessary that the occupant of the position be a man in perfect sympathy with the Secretary. Under these circumstances the Illinois Senators declared they would not think of pressing the candidacy of Mr. Smith. Lawrence O. Murray will be the next Controller.

At 10:58 the Secretary of Commerce and Labor comes in—Mr. Straus. Secretary Garfield is in the room The Cabinet as the chime finishes the Assembles fourth quarter. A distinguished-looking individual who has come in by the talisman of Baron Kaneko's name, and who begins by telling the President that he is not a Jap, although he has received two orders from the Emperor, wants to be an Assistant Commissioner for the Tokio Fair, but gets no encouragement. Francis B. Loomis, ex-Assistant Secretary of State, is to be Commissioner. Taft stalks in and takes his stand behind the chair at the right of the President's. Secretaries Root, Cortelyou, Metcalf, and Wilson, and Messrs. Meyer and Bonaparte, having come in something like that order, are all in place. Venezuela, the Berlin Embassy question, the Alaska situation, the revision of the anti-trust law, are on the tapis. It is just five minutes after the hour when the President takes his seat at the head of the council table.

GIVING AUDIENCES TO TWO HUNDRED

SATURDAY is a rainy day—a "growing day," the farmers would call it; oppressive, "muggy," in the Yankee vernacular. The weather is on everybody's nerves. Yesterday there was a prostration from the heat, and a Congressman shot a negro* to death and wounded a white man. To-day it is worse. Nobody is feeling himself. However, the President saw over two hundred people between 9:30 and 2:30, among the number being Senator Lodge, Senator Beveridge, Senator Borah, Senator Warner, Senator Overman, Senator Bourne, Mr. Justice Harlan, ex-Governor Allen of Porto Rico, the Government counsel of the Inter-State Commerce Commission, Secretary Taft [T.R.'s successor], Assistant Secretary of State Bacon, seventeen Congressmen, the United States Marshal of Mississippi, two newspaper correspondents, "Dry Dollar" Sullivan of New York, a Rough Rider, and dozens of others who have left no record of distinct personality upon my mind.

*The New York Times *reported on March 28, 1908, that Congressman James T. Heflin of Alabama shot and killed an African-American man on a Pennsylvania Avenue street car. The Congressman was on his way to a temperance lecture when he observed two men drinking from a bottle. They got into an argument and Heflin tossed Lewis Lumby off the car. He stated later that he thought Lumby reached for a weapon so Heflin drew and fired two shots. Heflin's first shot hit Thomas McCreary (a former jockey and well-known trainer) outside the car in the foot. The second shot hit Lewis Lumby in the head and he died later in the hospital. Heflin was charged with assault to kill and released on $5,000 bail (about $128,000 in 2015 dollars). Heflin was a proponent of implementation of Jim Crow laws segregating street cars and of white supremacy in general. The charges were dismissed and in subsequent campaigns, Heflin bragged of the shooting as one of his major career accomplishments.*

A brace of young lads were among those waiting in the Cabinet room before the doors were opened. They sat on a window ledge half an hour, their eyes dancing like a parcel of mice, till the great man of their dreams came in. He worked around to them in short order; they had plenty to say, and didn't want to go any more than he wanted them to go.

A Congressman from Northern New York had brought in several friends. The President detained them several minutes. "From up the State? By George, I am glad to see you! That's really my true home up there. It was you people who gave me my chance. In a sense I owe everything to you."

The President does not say "De-light-ed."

Then there was a man who had lately come from Africa, where he had done some lion shooting. "By George, you are the man whom I have got to see! You have been shooting lions in Africa. Come, now; tell me all about it. I am not going to let you go until I have heard the whole story. I am going down there the minute I get through with this!"—and the President dragged him off to the sofa, where the two sat half an hour discussing lion hunting.

To everybody the President talks Taft. To ex-Governor Allen he says:

"Taft is an ideal man. He's square. He wouldn't lend himself to anything not absolutely approved by his conscience for the sake of the Presidency. That's what I like about Taft."

The President grins when the ex-Governor tells him that he found the Porto Ricans easy people to deal with. "Of course," laughs the President, "there is less trouble in the island than there is in one vigorous American town."

It is a pleasing sight to see the venerable Justice Harlan and the young President. It is said the senior Justice is ready to resign, He has conceived such a regard for Mr. Roosevelt that it may be he wants him to appoint his successor. Whether or not this is the case, the interchange of ideas between the Judge, great-framed but stooped and hoary in the service of his country's constitutional interpretation, and the forceful personality who is accused of tearing the Constitution to tatters, is eager and, it would seem, affectionate.

"Oh! I am eager to have a good talk with the reformer and the—the—ornithologist," cries the President, as Judge Kohlsaat and Prof. Clark are ushered in. But it is Mr. Glasgow, counsel for the Inter-State Commerce Commission, whom he has sit down with him, and the

46

two are deep in legal papers before the scientist and the idealist have found seats.

The President addresses Timothy Sullivan gravely as "Senator" before the group in the Cabinet room, but when the eminent Tammany statesman is departing the President thinks of a practical joke (there may have been a little more to it than that), and calls out: "Tim! Oh, Tim; wait a minute! I want you to see a man who needs watching, a most unscrupulous person"—and sends for Assistant Attorney General Cooley, who comes in from the big mansard pile across the street, breathless, and sits down on the sofa with "Big Tim," while the President chuckles for five minutes at the scene. Mr. Cooley, a rather elegant person, and an idealist in politics, gets along very well with "Dry Dollar" Sullivan nevertheless. I don't know what they talked about.

Senator Owen of Oklahoma is an Indian, and he is a new man in the Senate, but he is the most forcible man with the most vigorous manner in tete-a-tete who has sat down with the President during the week.

Some pretty big things are going on, and the heads of two Washington newspaper bureaus have been admitted. The Secretary of War comes in and stands waiting until the President has given them two minutes apiece. The President won't allow the correspondents to quote him, but tells them frankly his position on the new anti-trust bill now before the Congress. He is in favour of it in principle, but he isn't sure about every provision it contains. He won't say he has not seen it, but he can't pretend to have had time to examine it. His position was made plain in his message. If the bill conforms to that, he is for it. One thing ought to be made clear: he won't stand for any legalisation of the boycott. Please make that clear. They had asked him not to use the word "boycott" at any rate. Therefore he is going to use the word "boycott." He won't stand for it under that or any other old name. There wasn't to be any misunderstanding about that, any possibility of a charge of double dealing. He couldn't interfere in Congress to the extent of protesting against the reference of the bill to any particular committee. He probably could say that it was time it came out of committee and was acted on.

Secretary Taft is greeted affectionately as "Big Bill."

A little friend of mine was very much scandalised the other day when I read aloud some autobiographical details of her childhood told by Queen Victoria in her *Letters,* just published. When the future Queen of England went to Windsor to see George IV, that monarch exclaimed, "Give us your paw!" A little later, as the King passed by with the Duchess of Gloucester in a phaeton, the little Princess caught his eye, and he cried, "Pop her in!" My young friend thought this most improper language for royalty. But the Queen's memoirs declare, in the very sentence following her quotation of the Georgian salute, that the King was a man of extreme dignity and charm of manner. Don't imagine because the President calls people "Bill" or "Tim," and employs sometimes very homely English, that any one undertakes familiarity toward him.

Senator Bourne of Oregon has been in again to-day, and finds it difficult to get the President's eye. While he is waiting, Representative Madden wins the President's sympathy for a bill appropriating $100,000 for the preservation of the cabin in which Lincoln was born. Half a dozen other callers are disposed of. Senator Bourne at last gets a few words. "Mr. Bonaparte will see you, Senator. Yes, I have talked, with him. See him for yourself. When? Very soon, I should think. In the next day or two. He was very reluctant about it. I doubt if he is willing. But he will talk with you." And the Senator from Oregon is pulled along by means of a handshake, and the next in line takes his place.

To one group of legislators the President speaks very forcibly on the necessity of repressing anarchism in this country. Defending for his order for the suppression of the anarchist journal, *La Question Sociale,* Mr. Roosevelt says with immense energy: "When—people— come—to—the—United—States—they've—got—to—BEHAVE— United—States!"

AN ESTIMATE OF MR. ROOSEVELT

HERE may be given, of course, but glimpses of the kaleidoscopic scenes enacting daily in the White House. These may serve, however, to give an idea of the manner in which the business of the Government is transacted and of the personality of the man who directs its transaction. So great is the natural public interest in this man, so unfounded have been some personal criticisms of him widely disseminated by the less scrupulous of his opponents, and in some particulars so incomplete has been the popular conception of his character, that it may be worth while to recapitulate here the impression which I formed of it while observing him as the centre of these scenes and many more. Any one who has read thus far may be depended upon to pardon the personal statement that the author has never been a partisan of Mr. Roosevelt. Besides a disposition to look with some contempt upon the Life Strenuous, the particular incarnation of the spirit of eager action exhibited in the person of Theodore Roosevelt had never commended itself to him as particularly admirable. He did not go to scoff, however; neither did he exactly remain to pray. He came away with an experience, however, which it may be to edification thus to relate. A week's close and constant observation of a man known but casually and publicly might reasonably be expected to modify a judgment. In the present case it wrought something very like a change of heart. The testimony is that of one whose name, of course, is of not the slightest consequence, and yet what any man, and especially one prejudiced against rather than in favour of Mr. Roosevelt, observed during rather an unusual opportunity, must be of some weight as a contribution toward a final estimate of the President.

He is, first of all, a physical marvel. He radiates energy as the sun radiates light and heat, and he does it apparently without losing a particle of his own energy.

It is not merely remarkable, it is a simple miracle, that this man can keep up day after day—it is a sufficient miracle that he can exhibit for one day—the power which emanates from him like energy from a dynamo. Once we all believed in a beautiful law known as that of the conservation of energy. No force, so went the dream, was lost, It only was transformed; it underwent metamorphosis; the sum of energy in the universe was always the same. It was the discovery of radium and the radioactive susbtances which wrought the discomfiture of that law. It is Mr. Roosevelt who discredits it entirely. He never knows that virtue has gone out of him. He radiates from morning until night, and he is nevertheless always radiant.

One despairs of giving a conception of the constancy and force of the stream of corpuscular personality given off by the President. It strikes the visitor directly the door of the Cabinet room closes behind him. It begins to play on his mind, his body, to accelerate his blood-current, and to set his nerves tingling and his skin aglow, as the Becquerel rays affect a sensitive screen. It is a healthy, pleasant influence, warming and awakening. It scatters chill and embarrassment; it restores equilibrium broken by the excitement of the prospective interview with a personage. I have once or twice remarked that young lads brought into the President's presence, after a clasp of his hand and a look stolen at his face, lift their heads and begin to talk fearlessly, to be dragged off reluctantly, waving their hands at their big friend. Repeatedly it was noticeable that the embarrassed spokesman of a delegation, stopping confused in his prepared speech, grinned back at the President's sympathetic laugh and began to tell his story simply and well. It is hard to make a set speech to the President—easy to talk to him straight away and from the heart; he draws it out of you; he bombards you with ever-flowing electrons of his energy and his personality.

Most callers at the White House are there for the purpose of bringing something away. The daily procession might be regarded as a constant raid upon the Presidential treasury of favours. Few of the raiders, it must be confessed, get away with much. Now, it takes energy to resist raiders. Mr. Roosevelt not only resists them and saves most of his possession from becoming their prey, but he manages to dispossess them of what little they have already and makes them ashamed of themselves for not having brought in more. The President's room is a place which has seen much spoiling of the

Egyptians. The President likes to give, and he does give, but no man with a greater genius for acquisition, the acquisition of information, ever lived. He has an infinite passion for facts; an insatiable thirst for information; he lays violent hands on any detail the existence of which he gets wind of. Every visitor pays him tribute. The President gives the visitor—possibly he gives him what he came for; if it be possible he does—but at all events he gives him a welcome, the sense that he has done well to come, and then he pumps him dry and sends him forth fulfilled of the President's own ideas, own opinions, and enthusiasm.

To watch this process going on hour after hour, day after day, gives one a sense of energy which he never suspected one human body could contain.

Never does the President appear to meet a personality than which he is not the stronger; an idea to which he is a stranger; a situation which disconcerts him. He is always master. He takes what he pleases, gives what he likes, and does his will upon all alike. Mr. Roosevelt never tires; the flow of his power does not fluctuate. There is never weariness on his brow nor, apparently, languor in his heart. To ennui he is a stranger—would be were he the humblest man in the land, tied down to its most commonplace labour. He is gifted with an eagerness of mind and a virility of body that would find excitation in any situation. I have watched the scientists at the Wood's Hole biological laboratory conduct investigations of fatigue; they measured by delicate machines the physical results of the wagging of a finger until it could wag no more; they observed the chemical changes that accompanied the beating of a turtle's heart. Mr. Roosevelt's most violent exertions would have given them no tangible results. It is to be presumed that catabolism ensues, but no evidence of it ever appears. The President ends the day as fresh as he began it. The wonder increases in view of the fact that he eats little. The pleasures of the table appeal to him not at all; he is notably abstemious in food and drink. Virility, vigor, vim, abound in him as in no man he meets, and their utmost exercise only increases the store. The President is a living illustration of the possibility of the miracle of the widow's cruse. He is a man of really phenomenal physical power, a fountain of perennial energy, a dynamic marvel.

It is my belief that a large part of the explanation of Mr. Roosevelt lies in this matter of his physical constitution. To what degree this is a gift of nature and to what degree an acquirement I do not know. His remarkable control of his energy, however, is certainly his acquisition. For the second striking fact about Mr. Roosevelt is this: That his dynamic outflow, inexhaustible as it appears to be, is yet directed with the strictest economy. I mean to say that not a particle of his energy is wasted. At every moment it is brought to bear in full current upon the particular object of the moment. This is what I mean:

The President is able to concentrate his entire attention on the subject in hand, whether it be for an hour or for thirty seconds, and then instantly to transfer it, still entirely concentrated, to another subject. Let me say that there is no subtlety in my observations, in my analysis. These are not the conclusions of a mental expert; they are not ingenious revelations of obscure phenomena or processes—they are simple statements of facts apparent to anybody who has the opportunity of seeing the President for a few hours—statements of facts not only apparent, but commanding. If the President's energy is phenomenal—and the whole world knows that it is—so is the mobility of his energy; so is the nimbleness of his mind. Swiftly and easily he passes from one thing to another totally disconnected with it. He flies from an affair of state to a hunting reminiscence; from that to an abstract ethical question; then to a literary or a historical subject; he settles a point in an army reorganisation plan; the next second he is talking earnestly to a visitor on the Lake Superior whitefish, the taste of its flesh and the articulation of its skeleton as compared with the shad; in another second or two he is urging the necessity of arming for the preservation of peace, and quoting Erasmus; then he takes up the case of a suspected violation of the Sherman law, and is at the heart of it in a minute; then he listens to the tale of a Southern politician and gives him rapid instruction; turns to the intricacies of the Venezuela imbroglio, with the mass of details of a long story which everybody else has forgotten at his fingertips; stops a moment to tell a naval aid the depth and capacity of the harbour of Auckland; is instantly intent on the matter of his great and good friend of the Caribbean; takes up a few candidacies for appointments, one by one; recalls with great gusto the story of an adventure on horseback; greets a delegation; discusses with a Cabinet secretary a recommendation he is thinking of sending to Congress. All this within half an hour. Each subject gets full attention when it is up; there is never any hurrying away from it, but there is no loitering over it.

The White House atmosphere is charged with energy, but there is no sense of haste. I think no visitor ever leaves with a feeling that he has not had ample time. There is plenty of time for everything, but every moment of time is used. Plenty of leisure even to stop and to tell a story, or hear one, but not a moment without something doing. I cannot imagine the President replying as Dionysius the Elder replied when asked when he would be at leisure, "God forbid that it should ever befall me." He might well, however, make the remark which Plutarch credits, I think it is to Epaminondas, "How came he to have so much leisure as to die, when there was so much stirring?" Mr. Loeb or an assistant secretary slips in now and then with a matter which can be disposed of by a word or by a stroke of the pen. The amount of routine business disposed of thus casually by the President during the day is enormous. But there is nothing casual in the President's treatment of the subjects to which he really addresses himself. It may be only one minute or two, but it is not an animadversion—it is entirely concentrated consideration. The President's power of attention is flexible, plastic, fluid.

Furthermore, it is not a transfer of attention only which the President achieves. It is a transference of interest and of sympathy. He enters into the new subject with his whole being. His manner changes; his pose alters; his language takes new colour. One could almost guess the subject under debate by the President's attitude, look, and tone of voice. With a boy he is a boy; with a Senator, a statesman; with a politician, a politician; with a diplomatist, a ruler; with a bunch of cattlemen, a ranchero; with a family, a father. I might illustrate this, endlessly, but this article already grows too long. The best summing up of this peculiarly vivid sympathy of Mr. Roosevelt's has been made by one who has seen him in many situations: " When he is at a funeral, he acts like the corpse; and when he is at a wedding, everybody takes him for the bride."

That is it precisely; the President enters into every situation with all his sympathy, all his heart; and his sympathy is catholic in the extreme. He has himself experienced many sides of life, and he has mingled freely with men and women who have drawn him in imagination into many more. His human sympathy is as wide as was that of Terence. It is altogether impossible, for one who observes the manner in which day after day he meets men of the most diverse fortunes, occupations, and tastes, to put down the President's attention to them to anything but sincere interest. One is not on his oath when he greets a caller, any more than when he is composing an epitaph. Fools, babblers, and bores come to the White House. They are swiftly dealt with. But as a rule the President is genuinely glad to see his visitors. He would be a most unhappy man in seclusion. When he is alone he falls back upon the companionship of an author—though I daresay he feels the disadvantage of not being able to talk back to him. The President is the omnivorous reader, pulling a book from his pocket when he has a moment unoccupied, and culling its ideas with the swiftness of a trained reviewer. Mr. John Burroughs, than whom no man has a juster knowledge of the President's character, dwells with amazement on this faculty.

His knowledge of standard literature is considerable; of contemporary writing, phenomenal. He has made his own the literature of several fields of history, and is more or less an authority on more subjects than American zoology and Irish mythology. But what I particularly noticed was his wide familiarity with the latest books and magazine literature—my own particular concern. In his reading the President exhibits that breadth of interest and sympathy which is observable in his dealings with his visitors. Life and the world in every one of innumerable phases, the multitudinous deeds of men, their thoughts and ways attract him with indescribable fascination; the physical facts concerning the habitat of man teem for him with vital importance. I should not imagine that his mind often enters the worlds of poetry or romance. He is allured rather by what is tangible. After a fashion, he respects sentiment—but the sentiments he indulges are those common to most men. He is not constituted to originate or to respond easily to unusual or subtle sentiments. The niceties of speculation or analysis would be likely to annoy him. Of robust moral fibre, ethical refinements make little appeal to him. It does not occur to him that man has no right to kill beasts for pleasure. He is not a contemplative man; he abstracts the immediate practical significance from a fact, but he does not pursue it and investigate its relationships for the purpose of any philosophy. He lives in his front rooms. Origins and ultimate conclusions interest him little. The world questions do not knock at his doors. Dreams do not nest in his heart. He requires only a basis upon which to act. He is a President, not a philosopher. The native hue of resolution is not in Mr. Roosevelt sicklied o'er with the pale cast of thought; nor do enterprises of great pith and moment, their currents turned awry, lose the name of action. With a humane breadth of knowledge and sympathy that would fit out a dozen poets or philosophers, he allows no urbane refinements to paralyse his power of performance. He is Spartan, not Attic.

To dwell for a moment on the President's capacity of sympathy: It is quite true that he is a man of strong opinions, that he believes in himself and is of iron will. That he is sincere in his interest in other men of whatever station in life or of none I am sure no one could observe him for a week and doubt. He does not merely send his humblest visitor away with the feeling that he has met a friend and exchanged ideas with him, but in a surprising number of cases he remembers that humble visitor, recalling a day or two later some remark that passed between them. What he learned from the visitor I believe the President never forgets. I hate to play Dr. Watson's part to the President's performances; I hate to be forever using the words "marvelous," "phenomenal," "extraordinary." Yet it is a literal fact that in several physical respects at least Mr. Roosevelt is a marvel—in, for instance, his abounding energy and his mobility of interest. It is once more necessary to resort to a strong adjective to characterise the amount of his information. He is master of a prodigious number of facts. If one is astonished at the end of half an hour with him, he is amazed at the end of a week. This man is ignorant of nothing—by which

I mean that there is nothing about which he does not know something; in most cases it is a good deal. Whether it be the character or antecedents of a candidate for an appointment, or the history of a piece of legislation, or the present status of a bill, or the date of a social movement or phenomenon in the West or the South or New England or in medieval Europe or in modern New Zealand, the name and date and work of an obscure author, or the plan of one˙ of Napoleon's battles, Mr. Roosevelt has information on it. Sometimes he is wrong—my observation was, not often. To dozens of visitors with whom I have heard him converse he recalls particulars of former meetings with them—some little incident, the names of three or four others who were there, the bully time they had had, the particular stories he had told and heard, the time his train left. In such details he was never mistaken. Greeting a man for the first time, he would tell him about his father or uncle, or give him some particulars regarding his own town. "What was your mother's name? Then you must be descended from Jonathan Edwards." Surprised assent is given. "I should like to have Jonathan Edwards for an ancestor. A long way back, though. He was a great man, but he had no sense of humour." There is really constant work for a Dr. Watson to stand by exclaiming: "Marvellous! Marvellous!" If the exigencies of political fortune should ever reduce Mr. Roosevelt to the necessity of seeking the means of subsistence in the ranks of the vulgar, he would do well as a practical clairvoyant.

Clairvoyant in a deeper sense is the President's knowledge of the contents of the popular mind and heart. I can only describe Popular Heart it so. No man in the history of our country, save Mr. Lincoln, has lived so close to the people, responded so instantly and so adequately to the popular sentiment, known so certainly what the people would stand for. I reluct from any attempt to interpret the President or account for him on any other grounds than those which showed themselves during the period the experiences of which this book describes. Nor is it necessary to do so. It is sufficient to watch Mr. Roosevelt in consultation with the official and unofficial representatives of the people who come to see him, to understand that he is indeed the type and ideal of the average American. He is not representative of the East. He knows that the centre of population has been for a quarter of a century in Indiana, and that it is likely to remain there for a century. A current magazine article describes the President as an ordinary man energised to the nth power. It accounts for him as an exhibition of complete normality. It makes other remarks about him which my observations refuse to confirm. But this they do confirm, and this, I feel free to say, the President's own estimate of himself confirms:

He has a peculiarly accurate, a quite phenomenally accurate, understanding of the average man. Mr. Roosevelt has said to me that he is no genius, that he does not recognise in himself the faintest scintillation of genius. In this he is over-modest. It is genius to understand the average man. To represent absolutely the average man, to contain within one's own soul all that is common to humanity, its common knowledge, instincts, hopes, fears, aspirations, and to contain nothing more at all, would be to be great beyond all other greatness. After all, common humanity is very wonderful and very noble. To be truly an average man would be to be a part of the mind of millions, to be possessor of the greatest thoughts that live in the world, to have a vision wider and farther-reaching than that of an isolated seer or poet whatsoever. It is the inalienable right of every free-born citizen to be an average man— and most of our fellow-countrymen have embraced that right and hold it sacredly. That is to say, in their good qualities they do not rise above the average, however short of the average they may be in others. Mr. Roosevelt is up to the average in every particular—he has the genius not to advance out of the understanding of the average man in any particular. He eschews, by instinct, the refinements of the idealistic reformer, the speculative philosopher. He never-allows the world of average men to catch him thinking in a suspicious manner. He knows to a nicety, he feels by means of a delicate sixth sense which the majority of us do not possess, precisely what the average man is thinking about or is ready to think about, wants or is ready to demand.

I have spoken of the curious contradiction between the President's democracy of manner and habit and his autocracy of performance. He is an autocrat, I take it, not in his own right, but in the right of the democracy. He is clear in his conviction that he knows what the people want, that he in his person represents the popular demand. It is clear enough, certainly, that he does not represent the ideas of the particular class in which he was born, nor of the education which was given him. It is in the confidence that he has behind him the will of the people that he asserts himself as no President before ever dared to assert himself.

This, however, is but one of the curious contradictions that go to make up the personality of Theodore Roosevelt. He is a mass of contradictions: An advocate of peace, he is a lover of war. He hastens to enlist for the Spanish war, he forces us to embark upon a great naval and military programme, and he makes a pet of the Army—but he of all the world stops the war in the East and he refuses to let the almost intolerable insults of a Castro nag him into a fight. He is a civil-service reformer—and a practical politician. And so on. The fact is, human nature is essentially paradoxical. Those are indeed singular and bewildering contradictions, which, on every hand, in every normal man, and in the Nation's ideal, are reconciled in the mysterious alembic of life.

Mr. Roosevelt is all the nearer the heart of the people just because he is not an academic theorist, not a bodiless abstraction, but a passionate, somewhat wilful, but wholly human, bundle of contradictions.

THE PRESIDENT ON MR. ROOSEVELT

I CAN imagine the President frankly discussing an estimate of himself such as the one recently published to which reference has been made. The President would be likely to say:

"An average man energised to the nth power? That's not far wrong. I am an average man. I am no genius. Nobody knows that better than I know it. I found that out long ago myself. I haven't a hint of genius in any direction. But it would be altogether wrong, it would be quite absurd, to say that I follow public sentiment and don't lead it. I do lead it; in any event, sometimes I lead it. I led it in the Panama action. We should never have had Panama without me. Nobody else would have got Panama. Nobody else would have dared to make the move I made. Nobody in the wide world. I did that, and public sentiment responded instantly and said that I was right. I am leading in the creation of interest in the regular Army and Navy. It is one of my pets to have the regular establishment well thought of, to bring it before the public attention and make the country proud of it. Nobody else would have dared do that. Nobody but me would have sent the fleet around the globe. I led in settling the anthracite strike. Who was it proposed all these things? Who worked the country up to them? The great movement to which the country is now aroused for the preservation of our National resources, am I following or leading in that?"

"I believe I have an unusual degree of sympathy with the average American, and understand him and what he wants better than my critics do. I meet here daily all sorts and conditions. I am not afraid of any of them. I know every man's subject pretty nearly as well as he does himself. I sympathise with the views of life, to some extent, of every one of them. I have a catholic sympathy. I don't know how I got it; I suppose I must have been born with it, although that sort of thing grows with the exercise. Try to understand men and enter into their lives, and you will soon be able to do it. These women who come here—it may seem to you a small thing, but they go away comforted. The mothers go away with a sense that the chief authority of their country understands something of their lives and of their troubles, just as the men who come—most of them have a home and a wife and children—go away feeling that I am a man just like themselves; that my family is a main thing with me too, and that I think about my children, and plan for them and worry over them too. I don't have to act. It flows out of me. I am interested. I can't tear myself away from one to go to another. They tell me how they feel and what they are interested in, and I tell them what I am doing and thinking about. I talk to them square, as man to man, every one of them. I haven't any reservations; couldn't have. I don't bullyrag them, either. I put my opinion just as strongly as I know how, but they like me for that. They wouldn't stand for being bullyragged any more than I would. They would detect the play-acting or insincerity mighty quick. Every man of them is full of interest to me. There was 'Dry Dollar' Sullivan a while ago. Tim has his good sides, and I can meet him on those good sides. He is a big man physically; stripped for a fight, he would show for a better man than I am, probably, but if we ever met he knows that it would be a mischief of a tussle, and that I would fight until I was blind. He has seen me by the ring-side, and he knows that I appreciate some of the things he is interested in. I believe he doesn't drink or even smoke, but in a way he likes his share of the cakes and ale of life. Most men do. So do I. Then there was the little Methodist preacher. In the essential things that he is interested in and stands for, in everything that is sincere and upright and making for righteousness, I am with him, and I guess he saw that."

"I know the common instincts of men. But I do lead. I don't follow all the time, for a fact. Lincoln had an almost miraculous understanding of the people. Not that I am to be mentioned in the same breath with Lincoln. Lincoln was an average man, but Lincoln was a genius besides—perhaps the only genius in our political history. They say that Lincoln followed, that he even didn't lead the country in the emancipation of the slaves, in the unyielding demand for the preservation of the Union. That is absurd. He furnished the arguments, put profound truths simply, prepared the sentiment, and then he led.

"Washington? Why, Washington didn't have a spark of genius. He was just the average man of his day, the very best type of his day with indomitable will, unbounded courage, and no end of faith, and no end of patience. No, I don't think he was a military genius at all. He fought away, and didn't know when he was whipped. Oh! He was a wonder, he was a hero for you! But it isn't genius that does big things. Washington was courage, determination, and patience raised to the nth power. That's why he is generally held to be the greatest of Americans. Frederick the Great wasn't a military genius. Not at all. Frederick ran away in his first battle. And his second and third battles were most commonplace exhibitions of soldiership. Then he began to win. Now an ordinary general wouldn't get four chances. He wouldn't have got a second chance after such a fiasco as Frederick's first fight was. He was a king, and could do as he pleased, and he kept plugging away at it till he learned the game."

"Have I got Washington's patience? Certainly I excuse you—put it at me. I hope I have; I think I have. Not Washington's perhaps, but still a good deal of patience. Let me see. I believe Washington had a temper, too. Can you imagine any one on this job who didn't have patience or who hadn't acquired it? Could any one see me here an hour without realising that I sometimes have to hold myself in? I know as well as any one that patience is power. I do possess it far more than I am given credit for. Here comes a bunch of reformers wanting me to break with the machine somewhere. People have always been at me to break with the machine somewhere. I have always fought it. I have never yet given into it on a matter of principle. But I have kept my temper. I have simply said, 'I am sorry you can't see it my way.' Why, from away back when I was Police Commissioner in New York I had to be patient and hold my tongue. They would have broken me in a day. Oh, no, indeed, I haven't always had my way. Not by a good deal. I understand compromise—when no principle is involved—and I understand waiting, too.

"People say I am impetuous, and hasty, and rash. Maybe I am. But they are usually mistaken in the specifications. I was called rash when I ordered the fleet around the world. Why, I had been planning that thing for over a year, and for six months the plans had been perfected, waiting the moment to put them into execution. They said I was impetuous when I sent my long message to Congress. Never in the world was there anything more carefully premeditated and timed. You see, there was danger of a reaction setting in. Strong efforts were being made to use the Wall Street troubles to discourage the movement for reform. I prepared that message deliberately, and timed its release to the hour. There was nothing impetuous about it. I wasn't goaded to it, and I didn't lose my head for a moment. I know the sentiment of this country; I know what the people want and what they ought to want, and I know the moment to say the word.

"Oh, I get a lot of fun out of it! I can't begin to tell you. I would be ashamed to let anybody know how much I enjoy the Presidency. I like to be at the centre of big things, and I like to give things. To refuse, though, is hard; I don't like that. Still, I am very happy. Plenty of work and a clear conscience ought to make any man happy."

Mind you, I don't affirm that the President said this. Only it is just what he might have said if it had occurred to him to discuss himself and his work.

For it is characteristic of the President that he has a very just conception of the character of Theodore Roosevelt.

THE END.

Get more great reading from BIG BYTE BOOKS